Following the Breadcrumb Path:

Navigating the Journey Toward God, Justice, and Love

Cedrick Von Jackson

Robert Ndung'u - Creative Artist

All rights reserved. This book is protected under the copyright laws of the United States of America. This book may not be reproduced in any form without permission in writing from the publisher or author, except in the case of brief quotations.

Copyright © 2013 Cedrick Von Jackson

Mimosa Tree Publishing Company

All rights reserved.

ISBN-13: 978-0-615-85440-3

DEDICATION

For my mother, Earline M. Jackson
"Silently She Slipped Away"

PREFACE

Rapper, poet J. Ivy says that, "We are all here for a reason on a particular path. You don't need a curriculum to know that you're a part of the math." The truth behind this is that sometimes we end up off the beaten path, traveling far from where we were meant to travel, searching for how we fit into life's equation. The poems and short stories included in this collection speak to my personal journey in life. Throughout these pages, you will be invited to walk with me down "The Breadcrumb Path," as I listen for the soft, still voice of God leading the way. You will be challenged to listen with me to the marginalized as they struggle to put together the broken pieces of lives that have been shattered by abuse, exploitation, and violence. And together, we will find encouragement in the fact that not only does true love exist, but it has the power to conquer and overcome.

While this is my personal journey, I have not traveled alone. You and I are connected. We have most likely traveled together, at some point along the way, haven't we? And if we haven't, you probably know someone who has walked this path, with whom these poems and writings will resonate, don't you? By all means, invite them, challenge them, encourage them to journey with us, following the breadcrumb path.

CONTENTS

Acknowledgments	i
Intro – In Search Of Finding	1
Part 1: Bread Of Heaven, Feed Us Till We Want No More	**3**
Broken Glass Everywhere	4
Whispers	5
Speak to My Heart – A Prayer	7
I Sat Alone	8
Restless	9
I Admit It – I'm Strange	11
Praying	13
Sweet Little Jesus Boy – All Grown Now	15
Easy Like . . .	16
Fishing On Sunday	18
Part 2: Breadcrumbs For the Master's Table	**20**
Are We Not More Than Birds	21
Untitled – Against Violence	22
For Jordan Shumate	23
So I Listened To The 9-1-1 Tapes	24
Ishmael To Abraham	26
At Least the Sun Is Shining	29
Watching Spoons	32
Black In Business	34

Miranda	36
Concession Speech	38
Tricking Daffodils	39
Beautiful Audacity	40
Part 3: Love Finds A Way, Leads The Way, Is The Way	**42**
If I Were To Write You A Love Poem	43
Amazing	44
For Lurrie and Ruthie	45
Old Friends	47
Haiku – For Yogi (My Wife)	49
I See Myself In You	50
Haiku – For Our Anniversary	51
Silently She Slipped Away	52
Sweetest Obsession	53
Some Things Are Just Nice	54
I Love That Beat	55
About The Author	**56**

ACKNOWLEDGMENTS

First and foremost, I thank God for the gifts and talents with which I have been entrusted. To God be the glory, who doeth all things well.

I thank my beautiful wife, Eulanda Kaye Jackson, for her undying love and support, not only with this project, but with all of those crazy ideas and dreams that continue to pop into my head. I love you!

I thank my children, Jalise and Myles for their love and patience with me as I write and minister. Daddy loves you guys!

I thank my family, with whom I have learned to laugh, cry, and discuss "agenda items."

I thank those who served on my creative and editorial team during this project: Lisa Bennett, Rev. Dr. Valerie Bridgeman, Denise Evans, Rev. Earle J. Fisher, LaJuan Kerr Tallo, and Jaha Zainabu. Thank you for walking this journey with me and for providing insight that proved golden.

I thank Tierica Berry, the coach who "kicked my butt" to get this done and recognized that I actually "had something to say."

Special thanks goes out to the members of Mt. Zion Missionary Baptist Church of Sardis, MS. It has been through serving you that I have found a huge portion of my "voice."

"SO HE CRUMPLED HIS BREAD AND LEFT A TRAIL OF CRUMBS INSTEAD" - HANSEL AND GRETEL

IN SEARCH OF FINDING

We have been found
In search of finding
Thoughts rewinding
Reminding us that
Our place in this world
Is only revealed
When truth is unfurled
Truth in
A love that lasts
Beyond the vast vestiges
Of our past selves
We are more than trophies
Occupying dusty shelves
Me I must be
Myself most authentic
Thinking on these things
Hope for the hopeless
Voice for the voiceless
Speak up

No road map
No compass
No GPS

Yes
Skies too cloudy
To navigate by stars
We will not
Follow the drinking gourd
Not tonight
The Light will guide us
Path so dark
Yet walking beside us
Footsteps unsure
Feeling your way
As you sometimes must

Feeling no-ways tired
But all-ways wearied
Yet pressing on

Blind leading blind
Connected by Spirit
And common struggle
Follow the drumbeat
Of your own heart
It leads the way
To finding

PART 1: BREAD OF HEAVEN, FEED US TILL WE WANT NO MORE

BROKEN GLASS EVERYWHERE

There was the evidence, all over the floor, in a million scattered pieces – a family vase that had been passed down like Law for three generations. The instructions had been quite simple – DO NOT RUN IN THE HOUSE! And what did he find himself doing? The same thing any overly energetic six-year old boy would do – running through the house. But now, there he stood over the evidence that would convict him and him alone. There was only one other person in the house, and he could not place the blame on her, for she was the one who had issued the instructions. And there she stood. Three feet away. Arms folded in anger. Feet tapping a solemn rhythm. Head shaking disapprovingly from side to side. Eyes squinted in disappointed disbelief. He wanted to explain, but even in his six-year old mind, he knew that no amount of explaining would satisfy in this situation. *I should have listened. I shouldn't have been running.* He thought to himself. But it was too late to follow directions this time.

Silence in the midst of disappointment turns moments into years.

She walks away. Head still shaking. Apparently to retrieve the instrument of his punishment. Returning shortly with a dust pan and broom. In silence, she sweeps up the mess, the convicting evidence, the broken pieces. In silence, she returns to the kitchen and empties the broken pieces into the trash and then returns to where he is still frozen in his tracks. In silence, she bends down and lifts him from the place of his great transgression, holds him above the place where the broken pieces once lay, and whispers gently in his ear . . .

The vase is broken, but I'm glad you're ok!

Restore us, LORD God Almighty; make your face shine on us, that we may be saved – Psalm 80:19

WHISPERS

Your whispers have caught me off guard
In still night I hear them
Often in my deepest state of sleep
Sometimes just before I finally close my eyes
Surprise is you are whispering
In voice that cannot be heard with ear
But with heart to the point I sometimes
Cannot differentiate between rhythm
The rhythm of your whisper and
The rhythm of my beating heart
Whose pace has quickened
From excitement once again hearing
Hearing you whisper as it has now been
Quite a long time
So long I knew it was something
I had done by mistake
Hoping you knew but still wouldn't
Hold it against me
When I heard it I sighed my head shook wondering
Wondering what took long for me to hear
Your whisper in my ear again
Again my head shook in awe because naw
You didn't hold it against me
I am utterly amazed
That you would set aside time
To wake me from my deep slumber
Or make sure I had not fallen asleep or asunder
Before you whispered in my ear that you love me
Madly deeply freely unconditionally love me
Again I had to catch my breath and slow my breathing
To keep my beating heart from palpitating
Because I knew that I knew that I knew that
I had messed things up in an unfixable messing-up
Kind of way
You whispered it's ok
Once again your whispers have caught me off guard

I find it's hard not to whisper back
I love you madly deeply freely
But with condition
Even though it's not my mission I know me pretty good
I know that even though I'm not planning on it
It won't be long now before I mess up again
I just hope on some night in my deepest state of sleep
Just before I close my eyes I'm blessed with the surprise
Of your whisper which has once again caught me off guard

SPEAK TO MY HEART – A PRAYER

Speak to my heart, Holy Spirit.
Speak peace.
Speak comfort.
Speak wisdom.
Speak power.
Speak strength.
Speak encouragement.
Speak softly, whisper so that I am forced to listen closely.
Speak loud and booming so I don't get too comfortable.
Speak creatively so I can create.
Speak love so I can feel love in return.
Speak light that casts away darkness.
Speak truth that dispels lies.
Speak tenderly so I will know how to be tender.
Speak plainly so I will know Your voice.

I SAT ALONE

I sat alone and I heard a whisper above the roar. I heard hope speak in the midst of chaos. I heard peace speak from the far reaches of confusion. All the lies of who we are and who we were and who we always will be were dispelled by the truth that we will always be more than that. Love was heard above hate. Light was seen through the darkest darkness. We were comforted because in the dark we stumble, but in the faintest light, we dance. I sat alone and I heard in the whisper and in the hope and in the peace and in the truth and in the light, I heard you call my name and I knew I was not alone.

RESTLESS

I should be working
but my heart is restless
and with a restless heart
it seems that a wandering mind
is soon to follow
work is not a priority
unfortunate side effect
of a restless heart
a mind
a body
a pair of hands
a set of feet
not thinking
functioning
working
doing what and going where
they all know they should
all of them searching but not finding
not finding fulfillment
not finding accomplishment
not finding love and comfort
not finding duty and obligation
all of them in search of finding
somehow constantly failing
the eyes of the restless hearted man
only finding the next pornographic website
the arms of the restless hearted woman
finding comfort in the arms
of one not her own
the esteem of a restless hearted employee
searching for another career
the very heart of a restless hearted child
who finds more "love"
under the strong hand of a pimp
or in the familial setting of a street gang
than under momma's roof
the mind of a restless hearted preacher

searching through the archives
of previously preached sermons
because another side effect of a restless heart
might be spiritually stopped ears
that cannot presently hear
the voice of God with clarity
all of them in search of finding
and somehow constantly failing

And so we pray, "You have made us for Yourself, O Lord, and our heart is restless until it rests in You." Help us find Your rest!

I ADMIT IT – I'M STRANGE

Holy and Awesome God, I present this hand, this pen, even this ink to You as vessels for your service . . .

I write my prayers out
And the longer the prayer the better
Or worse
I hold my hand funny
Never learned proper pen position
It hurts
Reminding me of the sacrifice of prayer
And my sermons too
And I do so defiantly because
Some old-school preacher
Told me real preachers
Would never write down
A sermon because God
Speaks in the pulpit not
Behind a computer or typewriter
Let alone the fact that God
Spoke through a donkey
Go figure
And I dream in color
But sometimes in black and white
Or even shades of grey because
Life is not always as
Cut and dried as black and white
And sometimes I just get a whim
That I want to paint
Let alone the fact that
I haven't painted in twenty years
And even when I did so
On the regular
I wasn't that good at it
But I'm ok with that too
And sometimes I just want to
Sit at my computer and write
And I guess what comes out

Is really to be considered poetry
Even though some would
Disagree because it doesn't always
Rhyme and I have no rhyme or
Reason why I divide the lines
Where I do
I just divide them where it
Feels good to me because
Its my poetry and I will
Divide where I want to
Divide where I want to
And like I said
It doesn't always rhyme
But that's still ok because
Wisdom cannot be contained
By rhyme patterns or confined
Within the scope of 16-bars

PRAYING

The prayers of the righteous
Availeth much
So tell me
Is it asking too much
For you to pray

Not the
Child I'm praying for you
At least that's what I said prayer
Just so you can
Get me out of your face prayer
Guilty - I've prayed that one too

But the prayer the real prayer
The show how much you care prayer
The down on your knees
Face to the ground prayer
Deep guttural sound prayer
The heavy sigh draw nigh unto God prayer
That can only be translated by Spirit prayer

Not the quick fix smoke and tricks prayer
Holy cloth sacred swath prayer

Not the Pharisees
Long words flowing phrases prayer
Not the standing on street corners
Collecting gazes prayer
I admit I was showing off

Not the Heavenly Father here I am
Knee bent body bowed
Before thy throne of grace prayer
But the Father AND Mother
I stretch my hand to Thee
No other help I know prayer

Would you pray if I asked you to
Or find something better to do
You pray for me
I pray for you
Cause I sure do need you to
And I'm not asking anything deep
I'll take now I lay me down to sleep
Long as you keep sending up timber
And remember my name in prayer

SWEET LITTLE JESUS BOY – ALL GROWN NOW

Sweet little Jesus boy
All grown now
Still unknown
Weight of the world shouldered
No white majestic stallion
Instead meek and lowly colt
Bearing you as you bore our sin
People rejoicing misunderstanding
Why you came
Shouting not knowing why
Save us mostly from ourselves
Save us they cried

Say to Daughter Zion, "See your king comes to you, gentle and riding on a donkey, and on a colt, the foal of a donkey." Matthew 21:5

EASY LIKE . . .

What's so easy about Sunday morning
The hallelujah is quite simple
Simple as parted lips
And uttered speech
It's the living after the shout
That can be complex

Living in delicate lipstick moments
Painted on smile
Hiding the crookedness
The sadness
The pain
The Lord will make a way
Somehow

Woke up this morning with my mind
Going in a thousand directions
Looking for center
For fire shut up in bones
A miracle
A sign

Spit shone shoes
Walk easily carrying eggshell emotions
Confident
At least that's the image
Isn't it
This Sunday morning thing
This *Sunday Moanin' thang*

Hiding behind
Wide brimmed hats
Looking all
Synthia Saint James
Let everything that hath breath
Keep breathing

Dressed up in Sunday's best
Feeling Saturday's worst
Cologne drenched handshakes
That linger
Longer than you'd like

Mahalia and Martin
And them Kennedy boys
Helping swat away the heat
From a Word that came
Too close for comfort
Hit just a little bit too hard
You been a long LONG time coming
BUT CHANGE AIN'T HAPPENED YET

FISHING ON SUNDAY

As we were riding home from church this afternoon, I noticed a scene that so reminded me of something that I would frequently hear my grandmother exclaim as I was moving through my formative years. She had several of these sayings, as I am sure most grandmothers did. While it was storming, we were not allowed to talk on the telephone for fear that lightning would travel through the lines and strike us dead. During those same storms, we were instructed to "get somewhere and be still" because "the Lord is doing His work." These were just a couple of examples of wisdom my grandmother would drop on us as we were growing up. These, however, are not the teachings that came to mind as I was driving home this afternoon! Alongside the highway, I caught a brief glimpse out of the corner of my eye of some people standing along a creek bed (that's riverside for those not of southern origin). Some were standing on the bank. Others were wading in the water. All of them were fishing. On a Sunday. And suddenly, the thought of what my grandmother taught us jumped into my mind, hitting me like a ton of bricks – DON'T GO FISHING ON SUNDAY; YOU'LL CATCH THE DEVIL!

Laugh, if you must, at the simplicity in this apparent old wives tale, but what my grandmother taught us, at least for me, carries profound theological understanding, grounded in the Law given by God to Moses. *Remember the Sabbath day, to keep it holy.* Fishing on Sunday stands in direct opposition to this command and the implication that NO WORK was to be done on the Sabbath. That this is a day for rest. This is a day for communion with God. This is a day for worship. Certain things just are not allowed. No rescuing oxen from pits. No healing of withered hands. No fishing. At least, not on Sunday. And the punishment for such iniquity? The Devil wrestling for your minnow at the other end of your line.

I vaguely remember a story told in hopes of reinforcing this teaching. It was one of those "Once upon a time" type stories where unfortunately, my grandmother (somewhere in her youth or childhood) broke this rule and found herself trying to land *something* at the other end of her line. Of course, the sight of this something never broke the surface of the water, so she really did not know what it was. But whatever it was, it put up the worst fight she had ever experienced in all of her fishing life. Now, you and I both know that the something at the other end of the line was just an enormous fish, don't we? DON'T WE?

Of course we do!

    But I guess here is the real question. How many times have we found ourselves really wrestling against something, and we didn't really know WHAT we were wrestling against? We didn't know HOW BIG it really was. All we know is that we felt like we were in the wrestle of our lives. And the reason we were wrestling was because we went "fishing on Sunday." We did not take the time to rest. We did not take the time to honor God. We did not take the time to commune with God. And what we wrestle against may never break the surface of the waters of our lives, fully revealing itself to us. And this may not be such a bad thing . . .

PART 2: BREADCRUMBS FROM THE MASTER'S TABLE

EVEN THE DOGS EAT THE CRUMBS THAT FALL FROM THEIR MASTER'S TABLE – MATTHEW 15:27

ARE WE NOT MORE THAN BIRDS

and suddenly one day
my granddaddy couldn't gather
as the old men always had
perched on the window sill
outside the general store
because the owner, mean, evil
cantankerous decided
to nail spikes in the space
my granddaddy and other old men
like him had gathered for years
as if my granddaddy was the bird
the storekeeper feared would
make a mess outside his store

UNTITLED – AGAINST VIOLENCE

Our eyes were watching but we did not see
The violence that transpired
The hearts made to bleed
Lives destroyed and dreams have been crushed
All because our voices remained hushed
Teddy bears and night lights
Won't keep the monsters at bay tonight
Because the real monsters do not hide under their beds
Instead images of the real monsters
Have been burned into their heads
And so sheets pulled tightly won't protect them nightly
Because when punches fly they still meet their targets
And with every blow a child's star gets dimmer
And if there is to be a glimmer of hope
Our eyes must see what has been before them all along
That our children need us to be strong
Not for us to strong-arm them
Recognize the call to hold not harm them
Using words to encourage not charm them
Into believing in false realities and fallacies
That good little boys and girls allow this but don't tell it
That a body does you no good unless you sell it
Well it gets deeper
Because it's not that our eyes could not see
But they saw and chose to ignore the truth right before them
And so the cycle continues
Where violence for some is the only choice on the menu
Violence begets violence and our daughters and our sons
Have learned in order to make it
You have to pack guns instead of love
And for them push has already come to shove
Growing up punching just like Daddy did
And taking it just like Mommy did
And in this cycle delayed dreams become denied dreams
And denied dreams transform into destroyed dreams
And it would seem that no dream needed to be crushed
If only our voices had not remained hushed

FOR JORDAN SHUMATE

Exactly what do you mean when you say
That you want me to read it blacker
Surely you must mean blacker as in
Articulate like my President or Martin or Malcolm
Or maybe your definition of blacker takes into consideration
The poetic flow of Drs. Angelou or Giovanni
Or countless other poets
Whose words may never become published
But are none-the-less potent and powerful and piercing
Life changing and system challenging
Or perhaps you mean blacker as in
The melodic sharps and flats on a baby grand
Without which hardly a concerto can be composed
Do you mean blacker as in the beauty of the blackest night
That is absolutely necessary in order for the stars
To have a contrasting background against which to shine
Or blacker as in with the brilliance and genius of those
Who performed the first heart surgery or designed the traffic light
Or blacker as in wonderfully rhythmic as an Alvin Ailey composition
Carefully choreographed by Jamison
Exactly what do you mean when you say
That you want me to read it blacker
Surely you must mean Crispus Attucks blacker
Revolutionary bold and heroic or maybe even Harriet Tubman blacker
Liberating and leading and I know
That this sounds like a lesson in history
But exactly how black do you need me to be
Would that be onyx blacker – precious and desired
Or airplane black box blacker sturdy and hard wired
What exactly do you mean

SO I LISTENED TO THE 9-1-1 TAPES

First of all, let me say that this, in no way, will be poetic.
At least not in the rhythmic, rhyming sense of being poetic.
So if you find a poem therein, it is purely coincidental.
And so, I listened to the 9-1-1 tapes and was painfully reminded
That injustice anywhere is a threat to justice everywhere.
And I am fearful for everyone who dares to walk "black" and talk "black"
And even live "black."
I am fearful that if justice is not now served,
Young black men will forever be shot for crimes
No greater than carrying a pack of skittles
And a can of commercially sold tea.
I am fearful that,
Just like we can ascertain from Mr. Zimmerman on the tapes,
Minds will already be made up about who I am,
What I am capable of, or not capable of.
And in my opinion, you should get to know me
Before you try and judge me.
Or better yet, how about you just get to know me
And leave the judging to the only One worthy and capable of judging.
And so, I listened to the 9-1-1 tapes and was painfully reminded that the
Cries of the innocent so often go unheard or ignored.
I was reminded that the sound of a gunshot in the middle of the night
Silences more than just a screaming voice.
It silences the beating of the hearts of those listening.
I was reminded that when a mind is already convinced of guilt
Based on the fact that "He just looks like he's up to something,"
Someone will always look like they're up to something,
And therefore forever be declared guilty
By the very ones who should be standing trial.
And what in the world does a neighborhood watch captain
Need to carry a 9mm for in the first place?
And what exactly is it that "They" always get away with?
And who exactly is this "They" that you speak so negatively against,
That get away with so much?
Because when I listened to the tape,
"They" were minding their own business.
And they didn't have a gun?

And they were crying out for help.
And they had a future snuffed out.
And they had a crowd of on-looking and on-listening neighbors
Who were horrified at what was being done to "They." I mean THEM.
And all of these neighbors had to have wondered when
"This" would happen to "Them," because surely
THIS could not happen in OUR neighborhood!
But it did! And so, I listened to the 9-1-1 tapes and
I could not help but notice that, as much as I hate to admit it,
Racism still exists in the hearts of the wicked.
And the wicked still press their case.
And I listened to the 9-1-1 tapes, hoping that justice would prevail,
And knowing that vengeance is mine saith the Lord,
And believing that we've come a long way,
And understanding that there is so much further to go!
I listened, and I was more than scared; I was horrified.
I was more than worried; I was disturbed.
I was more than mad; I was moved!
And this is not a poem. It is more than that.
It's a protest. It's a petition. It's a plea.
A plea that justice will be served.
That guilt not be pardoned.
And that none of us who heard the tape find ourselves on tape
For the same nonsense at the hands of which this young man died.

ISHMAEL TO ABRAHAM

You were more like
Biological didn't bother
Than father
And for the life of me
I never understood why
For a decade and some change
I find it strange that
I was your pride and joy
Your hope
Your promise of a future
Your proud progeny
But now I know
Nothing but abandonment
My sage bush
Bearing striking resemblance
To dumpsters
Into which
Children have been carelessly
And callously cast
My water-skin and bread
Running out as if
The child support check
Suddenly ceased
And your undiagnosed schizophrenia
Now causes me to pause
And wonder
To which voice were you listening
The day you sent me away
Now I am supposed to become
The father of a great nation too
But how can I
With these seeds you planted
These lessons you taught
Don't get me wrong
I know I'm blessed and highly favored
After all I am the first born son
But really

How was I to learn
The value of human life
When it seems you don't
Value it yourself
How was I to learn
Faithfulness in relationships
When you treated my mother
Like the side chick
Pumped dumped thrown away
How was I to learn
Unconditional love for my children
When you've been playing favorites
Ever since my brother was born
Was I to learn that a real father
Always provides for all his children
When you sent me away with nothing more
Than a prisoner's lunch
How long was this bread and water
To last anyway
I must say you've taught me a lot dad
But the most important lesson
That I've had is this
I've learned the bitter sting
Of being loved one moment
And rejected the next
I've learned the joy of being thrown in the air
Only to come crashing down
And suddenly thrown away
But most importantly
I've learned that my sons and daughters
Will not learn these same lessons
At least not in the same way
At least not from me
You see I will teach them
To always make sure
It is God's voice that they hear
And not some jealous individual
Whispering in their ear
They will learn that
They are not replaceable

Like burned out light bulbs
That have lost their luster
They will learn that
They will not be forgotten
Like Sunday School memory verses
And when they say their
Now I lay me down to sleeps
They will sleep well
Because I have already
Loved them so tightly
They will feel it all through the night
This they will learn because
I chose to be a father
When you kind sir
Did not even bother

AT LEAST THE SUN IS SHINING

On days that
Sun shines while rain showers fall
My grandmother would say
The devil is beating his wife

And I wondered what did he say
To make her stay
These tears from heaven
Drenching the Earth like rain
Were outer signs
Of her inner pain
And we looked on in delight
Because at least the sun was shining
Right

Ignoring the thunder of her cries
The subtle wind of her sighs
Because at least the sun was shining
Right

That's just thunder
That's just wind
We've heard it before
We'll feel it again
At least the sun is shining
Right

Ain't no sunshine when he's gone
Is a lie
And the longer she stays
The less likely she is to leave
A relationship that's built on lies
She's been forced to receive
Bound to the chains
Of a toxic relationship
By the hands of a false god
Who endorses

Covenant made before her people
Above the sanctity of her life
That's not the God I serve
Bound by the belief system of a people
Who hold that
The ability to persevere through pain
Is the mark of a good wife
Don't piss on me and tell me it's raining

And don't get it twisted
She's tried to leave before
But every time her trembling hand
Reaches for the door
He feeds her with more lies like
I'll never do it again
I love you unconditionally
I've made a change
We can make this work

And when that set of twisted lies fails
There's another sordid set of lies he tells

You'll never make it without me
I can't make it without you
Your kids will never speak to you again
And what will your mother say
If this doesn't work

Control manipulation
Demands and stipulations
Go unseen
Because love covers a multitude of sins
But then again
Is it really love

Her bills are paid
There's a roof over her head
She knows she should leave
But she stays instead

And she cries
And the sun shines
And the rains fall
And we look on in delight
Because after all
The sun is shining
RIGHT

WATCHING SPOONS

And the guy at the counter
Said they sure made the
Coffee strong this morning
See it holds up my spoon

And I guess I'm supposed to laugh at that
After all it's an old trick
And we've been trained to
Always laugh at old tricks haven't we

And you could tell he was an old dog
Old dog hat and slacks
Old dog shirt and suspenders
Still performing old dog tricks

And we're supposed to still be laughing
But it is no longer funny – these old dog tricks

This ancient slight of hand
Tricking Natives out of their land
This smoke and mirrors across the nation
Trading test scores and degrees for real education

And we've been trained to focus on the spoon
Real tricks carried out in back rooms and board rooms
Access denied held under lock and key
Removing the man from manifest destiny

And we've been trained to focus on the spoon
Shoot for the stars aim for the moon
Somehow missing them both
And ending up with only darkness and a little dust

Say something to the man son
You like ball son – yeah
Say yes sir
Yes sir

Well you've got a future son
Long as you keep ballin' son
One day you'll make it son
Agents will be callin' son

But while you're dribbling they're dealing
And while you're pulling cross-overs they're concealing
Your real worth – not in the capers you pull on court
But in the other dreams they helped you abort

While you were spoon watching as a matter of fact
The real trickery was happening behind your back
Smoke and mirrors and even spoons only distract
When you are the object of the vanishing act

BLACK IN BUSINESS

Do not take my words to mean that
I have all of a sudden become a militant radical
I raise not a clinched fist but an
Ebony hued symbol of peace
Two fingers heavenly aimed victoriously proud
Do not take my words to mean that
I will continuously shout from the mountain top
That the world system has stifled my dreams
I have awoken myself from that slumber
And now perpetuate my own dreams
Fully combustible igniting the dream fire
In others regardless of their skin tones
Do not take my words to mean that
I have taken on the family stigma
That my highest expectation for myself
Is to push the phattest ride on the
Most expensive rims with the latest candy paint
While we wine and dine on the banquets of foodstamps
Do not take my words to mean that
I plan to stand in silent stupor while
While injustice plays out on our city streets
And in our city courts and
Beneath white-washed steeples
While the lie is propagated that God is color-blind
And yet racially skewed toward the color green
Do not take my words to mean that
I am just fine with the assumption that
I am inherently born with the rhythm of a rapper
Or with the jig of Bojangles or with Owen-esque speed
Why not equally assume that I am
As classic as Beethoven or Coleridge-Taylor
Do not take my words to mean that
When you look at my business means
You will find difficulty in distinguishing my wares
From the wares of Johnson & Johnson
I handle my business in the boardroom
And in the classroom not on the triple-beam

Do not take my words to mean that
Do not take my words to mean that

MIRANDA

I do not have the right to remain silent
I have the right to raised voice
To protest to speak out
To speak life and
Condemn death and hate
I have the right to say
You were wrong and
So was I
I can admit my own guilt
My own part played
Can you
I have a right to scream justice
Shout injustice
Proclaim foul play
To speak by raised fist
By lifted fingers
V-style
To proclaim peace and
Deuces, I'll holla
At same time
I have a right to cry out
For Trayvon
For Chicago
For Marissa Alexander
For Darius Simmons
And for countless others whose name
You'll never know
Because you chose to ignore issue at hand
Yes I have a right to cry out
It's my party . . .
It's our party
But ain't nobody having fun
Ain't no dancing
Only shucking and jiving
Ain't no music
Only voices crying out
I have the right to scream racism

From both sides of the street
My side
And the other side
Because as quickly as others
Want to grab their purse tightly as I walk by
I too sometimes want to give you
An assumed reason to do so
I don't want or need your purse
Got a job
A good paying one
I have a right to say
That's a stupid law
I know it's law but it's still stupid
And just because I must live by it
Doesn't mean I can't vote to change it
That's the ground I stand
These are my rights
And many more
But I do not have
The right to remain silent

CONCESSION SPEECH

my fellow citizens, on this cool somber eve
i stand before you, God, this nation
offering a disparaging note of concession
we have fought a long and arduous battle
scars and wounds are evident on both sides
but every good fight must come to an end
and so this one finally does
we concede to the powers and principalities in high places
that have convinced us that while wages are still
determined by gender, skin color, and cultural background
we live and operate on a level playing field
we concede to those who continue to perpetuate the belief
that every homeless person walking the street
is there by their own recognizance or fault
that there is an opportunity for them to make it
that those walking main street had the same
opportunity of those walking down wall street
we concede to those who believe that we are moral enough
and righteous enough and trustworthy enough
to become the royal mounted police for the entire world
we concede to those who would dare say that
racial profiling does not exist but equal health care does
we concede to those who shift their own paradigm
for whenever it seems most appropriate to them
our list of concessions is far too lengthy to continue
and so to those who have fought along side us
i say to you thank you
our concession does not imply
that our voices have not been heard
that our issues have not been raised
that our opinions have not mattered
they have
and so while we may concede the fight
on this cool somber eve
we still know the truth
and the truth hurts

TRICKING DAFFODILS

We go about this business quite easily
Like tricking the daffodils
Into early emergence
Promising hope of warmth
Only to be frozen stiff
By winds of change and disbelief
And so we wait until April to cry
Because tears can be hidden better
By Spring showers
Than by Winter snowfall

BEAUTIFUL AUDACITY

I stepped outside into the beautiful
Post-storm sunlight and could not help but
Notice that a beautiful black butterfly
Had the beautiful audacity to take flight
Expressing a freedom that said I WILL take flight
Not knowing when the next
Prevailing contrary wind may rise up

And I thought to myself there is a lesson message sermon
In there somewhere
I was created to take flight
I was created to spread my wings
Against the prevailing winds and dare to soar
Not knowing where the breeze would take me
Not having a care in the world
But to ride it out and see where I end
Understanding that by carefree flight
I am fulfilling part of my purpose
Which is to let others see just a glimpse
Just a glimpse of beauty no matter
What the storm that was just recently encountered
Did to the world or even to me
I was created to soar above
Above what the storm could not destroy
Even though it tried with all of its might
It left evidence of the attempt
It was greatly reported
And yet we are still here all of us
Butterflies daring to take flight against
Prevailing and contrary winds
Our purpose to show that even after the storm
There is beautiful audacity
So after Katrina Rita Andrew Elvis
And countless other nameless storms
There is beautiful audacity
After A.I.D.S. Cancer Chemo Hunger
There is beautiful audacity
After homelessness violence fear injustice

There is beautiful audacity
After bigotry hatred pestilence WAR
There is beautiful audacity
We will prevail against what seeks
To prevail against us
We will take flight against and above
That which seeks to hold us flightless
Flaunting our beauty daring the beholder
To say otherwise

PART 3: LOVE FINDS A WAY, LEADS THE WAY, IS THE WAY

IF I WERE TO WRITE YOU A LOVE POEM

If I were to write you a love poem
It would be musical
And we would no longer make love
We would make largo
Slow and steady
Sultry and sweet
And from high above the heavens
In the place where Cassiopeia and Orion
Play coy like star-crossed lovers
We would be eternal
And when we stride through the woods
The cottonwoods would applaud our arrival
Cypress trees would bend their knees
Praying our love would last
And mimosas would sleep easy
Knowing our hearts and hands
Were intricately intertwined
I would shout sweet everythings
To the corners of the world
Because in love whispering is for cowards

AMAZING

You are
Not because of your strength
But because you don't mind
Letting your weakness show
Not because you dance so well
But because the only rhythm that matters
Is the beat of your own heart
Not because your voice is melodic
But because it speaks truth to power
Not because of popularity
But because you dare to live out loud
Not because you know all the answers
But because you have the ability
To formulate your own questions
And dare others to find the answers
Not because you always find yourself
On the side of the winner
But because you fight on
In spite of defeat
Not because of the number of loves
But because of the quality of the few
Or even the one
Not because others proclaim your amazingness
But because you just are

FOR LURRIE AND RUTHIE

It was all in the look
The look that said
I've been here for
More than fifty years
And I'd be here for
Fifty more if you allow
Right by your side
The look that said
You're still my honey
And I'd say I do
All over again
If you'd only ask
The look that said
Don't leave yet
But if you do
I'm coming too
So you bet' not leave
Because I can't come
Where I know you'd go
The look that said
I see you hurting
And it's hurting me
To see you
Hurting that way
The look that said
Baby thank you
For every meal cooked
And every bath run
And every baby's diaper changed
And for always seeing
Me as your man
The look that said
Sometimes you made me sick
But loving you
Was worth every minute
Of whatever sickness I felt
The look that said

I'd be lost without you
The look that said
Yeah me too
The look that said
I'm sorry
For every time
I caused you pain
Especially now
The look that said
It's ok
I forgive you
Especially now
That's how much
I love you
I hope you see it

OLD FRIENDS

We are old friends
Like ocean waves lapping on seashore
Old friends to the point that
I no more mind your interruptions
Than cloudless sky
Minds visitation from thunderheads
You are my
Put me in check
We are silent conversations
And blank stares that speak volumes
Double dutch in the rain
And pink cotton candy sticky fingers
We are patchwork quilt
Stitched together with old school love
Not always matching
But ever serving purpose and need
You are ripple that disrupts
The stillness of my ever flowing stream
You are my real
My concentric circles growing larger
With time
My honesty
My truth
I look out on your friendship
And catch glimpses of horizon
Going on
As far as eye can see
Anchors cannot fathom
The depth of our commitment
To one another
You are my strong shoulder
My cry
My wipe my tears away
We are phone calls at midnight
At two a.m.
And three a.m.
And four a.m.
And whenever I need

Minus the caller ID
And answering machine
We are
Never can say goodbye
Because every separation
Demands howdy howdy
Never goodbye

HAIKU – FOR YOGI (MY WIFE)

my constant heartbeat
my persistent metronome
dearly I love you

I SEE MYSELF IN YOU

. . . And no, this ain't no pick up line
Kind of baby you must be a mirror cuz . . .
I see myself in you
You shoulda seen the look on your face
And in your eye when I said that
But I see myself in you
In the way you walk – that's my walk
And when you speak you talk my talk
I can see the twinkle and surprise
In my own eyes
When I look into yours
When you frown
That's my own smile turned upside down
And when you smile
I can feel the me inside you turn
Flips, somersaults, cartwheels
I could see myself doing that
That thought you just had
That was my thought
I thought you knew
I was crazy but still
I see myself in you
And the way I drum your fingers
On the table still lingers with the idea
Of you in whom I see myself
I see myself in you
And no, this ain't no pick-up line
But still I see myself

HAIKU – FOR OUR ANNIVERSARY

I'll be your cello
If you'll be my violin
Background, piano

SILENTLY SHE SLIPPED AWAY

Silently she slipped away
While I stood there cold
A lonely stranger in a room
Crowded with family
Death the unwelcomed guest
We knew was coming soon
It took time
Time heals all wounds they say
Not really
Convinced I had cried my last tear
I found myself in this tear cycle
A couple of tears a
Couple of years later
A couple of tears a
Couple of years later
But I don't cry no more
Now I just sigh or laugh
Or whatever twisted emotion
Spirals its way from the
Depths of my soul
It's how I deal with it now
I will probably not be here
When you get back was
Never before so ironically true
Parting words are like that
Especially in the knowing
The soul always knows when time has come
Isn't that what they say
And now all I have left are
Pictures and precious memories
That will have to
Suffice in the clutch

SWEETEST OBSESSION

Sweetest Obsession
Be thou gentle with me tonight
Haunt me not
With taunting thoughts
Of unquenched desire
Allow me to erase memory
Of your never fading beauty
From far corners
Of my mind until the moment
I no longer need memory
But am privileged to behold
The splendor of the real you

SOME THINGS ARE JUST NICE

Like butterfly over ocean
Or gentle breeze
Fireflies fluttering
So high they become
Confused with stars in
Nighttime sky
Like finding a new friend
At thirty-two thousand feet
If only for a brief jaunt
To the islands
Cease fire in the midst of a
Verbally escalated war
Or knowing that you are
Known for just who you are
And it doesn't matter
Some things are just nice

I LOVE THAT BEAT

I love that beat like my heart pounding
Rhythmic, steady, racing
Keeping up with the pace of life
Sometimes palpitating, skipping
Getting off kilter I love that beat
Syncopated, dancing, staccato
Bouncing all over the place
Like the bouncing dot at the
Bottom of the screen guiding you
Through that song that you don't know
But sing anyway
I love that beat
Like the pitter patter of the rain
Falling, multi-tempoed, so complex that
You can't find the rhythm so that
Everyone that tries to dance to it
Looks like they're dancing to the
Beat of their own drummer
Some of them feel it – some of them don't
I love that beat
Coming out of the deepest darkest jungles
Exotic and trance inducing
More ancient than the trees from
Which the drums were hewn
Marching down through the ages
Like soldiers stepping to a
Drill sergeant's steady, barked cadence
Left . . . left . . . left . . . right . . . left
I love that beat
New Orleans jazz and zydeco
Ragtime and waltz, 1-2-3, 1-2-3
Foxtrot and Charleston
I love that beat
Find your own to love

ABOUT THE AUTHOR

We are all on a particular and peculiar path. Born in Memphis, TN and raised in Coldwater, MS, Cedrick Von Jackson acknowledges that his path has been guided by God and Spirit and shaped through the arts. As an ordained minister and Baptist pastor, he has published sermons and sermon illustrations in "The African American Pulpit" and at www.theafricanamericanlectionary.org. As an actor on the community theatre stage, he has performed in musicals like "The Music Man," "The Fantasticks," "A Chorus Line," and a special performance of "The Wiz" with Memphis Black Repertory Theatre and the Memphis Symphony Orchestra, as well as Neil Simon's "Proposals," and the hit "Driving Miss Daisy." Cedrick has been writing poetry for ten years, and can be found blogging at www.literallyced.wordpress.com.

www.ingramcontent.com/pod-product-compliance
Lightning Source LLC
Chambersburg PA
CBHW072015060426
42446CB00043B/2558